THE PAVESE STONE

THE PAVESE STONE

poems

JUDITH VOLLMER

ALICE JAMES BOOKS
NEW GLOUCESTER, MAINE • ALICEJAMESBOOKS.ORG

Printed in the United States

10 9 8 7 6 5 4 3 2 1

Alice James Books are published by Alice James Poetry Cooperative, Inc.

Alice James Books
Auburn Hall
60 Pineland Drive, Suite 206
New Gloucester, ME 04260
www.alicejamesbooks.org

Library of Congress Cataloging-in-Publication Data

Names: Vollmer, Judith, 1951- author
http://id.loc.gov/authorities/names/n90652953
http://id.loc.gov/rwo/agents/n90652953
Title: The Pavese stone / Judith Vollmer.
Other titles: Pavese stone (Compilation)
Identifiers: LCCN 2025024309 (print) | LCCN 2025024310 (ebook) | ISBN 9781967149087 trade paperback | ISBN 9781967149094 epub
Subjects: LCGFT: Poetry
http://id.loc.gov/authorities/genreForms/gf2014026481
Classification: LCC PS3572.O3957 P38 2026 (print) | LCC PS3572.O3957 (ebook) | DDC 811/.54--dc23/eng/20250613
LC record available at https://lccn.loc.gov/2025024309
LC ebook record available at https://lccn.loc.gov/2025024310

Alice James Books gratefully acknowledges support from individual donors, private foundations, and the Poetry Foundation (https://www.poetryfoundation.org).

Cover image: Head of a Young Woman, Unidentified (Italian), copy after Domenico Ghirlandaio, 15th century, fresco. Smithsonian American Art Museum, Gift of John Gellatly, object no. 1929.6.2. CC0 (Public Domain), via Smithsonian Open Access, si.edu/object/saam_1929.6.2.

for Ann and our families

TABLE OF CONTENTS

III.

I.

II.

III.

THE OWLS OF PIAZZA DELLA ROTONDA

—Living birds for sale:
nightingales and thrushes, parrots
and sparrows, all chattering and cooing.
Among them on stands and perches, may be seen all sorts of owls.
—William Story, *Roba di Roma*, 1864

I've seen her flutter and drop
for vole, once a clutch of mice,
watched her perch in the red spruce,
head locked on the alley. Once, dusk, a rat
rustled in the ditch and skittered the brick wall
to open window, to crib,
and chewed an infant's lips
to blood. Was she near?
I pray I'll see her again—
show me how to collapse the terrible distances
place to place, stretch into other lives
as I stare up into the Winter Hexagram's
six stars.
    Lonely human wishes
twist my head, I love her.
Some say the sole intelligence
of owls is the hunt, the feeding kill.
    Do you crave a five-grand
French bulldog, a star-fuck, a big prize?
    Then you understand
the piazza market and its wares,
women preening, strolling,

owls tied to their velvet wrists,
trophies. I offer my head-and-handwriting
    to her sky.
Who can see distance or save a thing,
fly that fast toward prey and food?

Deep violet and green
under the temple wing
hiding my face with shadows
and a knife in my sleeve.
Daybreak, no customers,
I cut the leather cords,
owls lift like tablecloths, feathers fanning
and whipping the flimsy ties.

Solemn *barbigiani;*
    white-tufted prince;
    little *civetta* (you heartless flirt);
and the *aziola*, Shelley's minor poem's
central character:

I felt to know it was nothing human

No one saw me approach or leave.
One last, old and slower,
I invited onto my shoulder.

Such as nor voice, nor lute

nor wind, nor bird,
the soul ever stirred

I swiveled my head and met her eyes,
and we flew.

THE TUBE

The week I moved here, barely unpacked,
someone slapped me fully in the face,
crossing a parking lot
coming from opposite directions,
threading through mopeds
and Smartcars, she was staring
and in the instant
passing each other, from less than
an arm's width came the slap. It didn't

hurt, a sting from a bat wing
or flying fish, I took it as a benediction,
like the row of cobbles on the left side
of my new street that point directly
to my corner and up my steps into my
front room;
                    one evening hour
that first week I saw
fastened to the wall,
roughly chair-rail height,

a glass tube
an inch or so thick, pulsing light around
the perimeter, like weird neon, or

I could say insect fluid, or liquid
chlorophyll stored for winter.
That light, that harsh palm
to my face—keep and deny
my solitude.
I am telling you this so you'll
not feel so lonely,
though I understand if you do.

ALONG THE JUNIATA

—for Peter Oresick, 1955-2016

The moon shifted, and figures ran across the wall

repeating back and forth, hatchwork

of human arms, a turnpike guardrail, spruce-trunks,

wind-shreds, then stopped, centered the room

floor-to-ceiling, and took the shape

of a slender river witch, dripping branches.

"I was expecting a face!" I shouted

in half-sleep, hot asphalt speed

roiling under me, my all-day drive

toward your dying.

Her branches scratched down onto my bed,

table lamp still burning,

then covered that too, all

but your book I felt

she'd come to read, or act out,

or translate to Rusyn,

or a primer of how a tree

might paint you,

strong brush-work of birch tincture

to anoint, alleviate

your last heaving.

SUGAR TABLE

—surely your road from this world
will cross a dessert table
—Tsvetayeva, tr. Elaine Feinstein

My hand slides
the linen cross-stitched roses,
nut horns and lemon creams,
palms two, slides down and away from
Baci's swatting hands that ironed the immaculate
tabularium she built in a day.
Butter clouds laminate the house.

In the fridge, chocolate drops
will stay waxy
and not melt
like Wujek's face on the satin pillow.
Now men come and snap the casket shut.

Process the snowy hill
tailed by violins. Strianka's black boot-tips
print snow, stab close, closer to the hole
she wails and slips into. Pull her back up,
please, lay her on our neighbor's
dry stone. She stirs, we resume,
violinists elbow the screeching
jays up onto the spruce.

*

Up the steps to the vertical world's repast,
boots track mud, coats drop onto beds,
violin cases lean in the hall.
Squeeze into the front room's two dozen chairs
and unfold for songs and talk.
I know if the rivers flow
so does the money. I scrape my teeth
across a cookie, men sing and tap.
Father Milano hands me another
I dip into my child-coffee
now that I am eight. *Father,*
what is the Holy Ghost? Murmur
of prayer, *Child,*
we live in mystery.
It is like a sliding door.

If the rivers flow, levels up, down,
money oils the locks. Rivers flow,
so does money, we spend it all up.
The men blend Seagram's 7 & 7, toss
Stoney bottles under the sink. Out
on the icy-cracked porch
aunts smoke and steal time
while the hot meal steams.

*

None had teeth.
Horseshoe-frames soaked in salt or soda,
Polident on payday. Lips and half-
chins and noses swallowed.

When they slid the frames onto glue
and clamped them back inside
they looked right again,
voices like twig-switches
kept time, swept time along the walls,
under the table, up and across tray after tray
emptying. Doilies ringed with butter.
I have never heard more brilliant talk
I could not understand:

broken English, fancy Polish,
dialog operatic or hatcheted,
vernacular. Spritzing dialect with school
English, all the geographic tongues
rough with the holy trinity:
food, shelter, drink. Voices
hoarse, sweaty faces
lit by first streetlights snapping on,
so witty and detailed, long tales
of cradle, table, the lascivious and the shy,
back-seats and wedding beds, blooded or not.

The men are singing about coal.
The Scots, the bastard Irish, bosses of us all,
levels up, levels down
they run the controls and the locks,
run the scrip, the coffee too,
we shovel the coal,
they own the rivers, the store, the house.

*

I retreat under the table, cradling
my thimble of wisniówka
rilling all the ridges

of my swollen gums.

Where the coffin rested on its trolley
overnight, the carpet is edged
in powdered sugar,

horizontal and applied, like love, with pressure.

LATE EXCERPT

Soon at your door a letter
you might lift to feel
the weight of my palm,

expecting remorse
or blame. Tossed
or composted, its inks

and glue will seep
into the Youghiogheny,
river that twists back on itself

then unwinds into the Mon,
then the aquifer holding its blue
body beneath my back porch

where we'd sit among moonflowers—
I still talk with you, now
that only the water is speaking.

COFFEE AND CLOTH

I.

Steaming cup lifts night, and I enter the brainwheel,
the pantry glows purple and orange,
plums and apricots. Stack of newspaper awaiting the bin.
Behind drywall the lathe warps and weeps.

When I can no longer move to that city
I transport its light strokes, first thoughts, river-froth,
cross-streets' tilting lungs. Dear kin:
what is a thought—a scent, a room, a novel's spine?

Cat thought might be bluejay brushing birdbath, leaving
water circles. Superior to Spiral Jetty or orange draperies
gating Central Park. Say I filed my teeth
on steel: now my bicuspids sharp at 70.

Auburn and silver my Baci's coiled braid,
her lips wrinkled as the goat's. Her eye cup glinted,
lens to the under-sink, cellar, cinder layer,
Earth. Four-gallon blue-speckled pot of A&P

fine-grind plenty for four days' labor, watered to stretch.
Men up at five, back before *zmierch*/dusk, her quiet hour,
wrapping boxes in burlap, stitching
her sister's Krosno address in fine black thread,

sealing with hemp twine. White socks and Ben-Gay,
housedresses, bras, ghosts of books she could not read.
I once saw her tuck one of her own dress designs in:
salvaged lace, silk lining, blue satin French knots

studding white organdy, *załóż to*
na ślub Anthony ego/wear this for Anthony's wedding.
Eight slept in her three upstairs rooms, a wealth
she dreamed would one day be hers, wealth I stitch

through *kawa,*
and goblets of wine, superior to hashish,
both Baudelaire and Shelley wrote. About coffee or cloth
neither is expert. On sugar, Leopardi is terse: "It is not

a simple substance." In my re-reading
I see places expand, but need
more focus. Passageways sink, soul-tired,
Rich's dream-dictum "When the estrus goes it takes the vile"—

nice idea . . . Labels rot and roll through my lathe. I love
the moka pot, the Mr. Coffee, French press, plastic filters w/paper,
dented Napolitano, scratched glass percolator. I failed
four online IQ tests and the death-path beckons, but resins

and fibers lead me. I have always mostly thought of
koffie every night anticipating first cup. That chemo
year I was glad espresso was still on the menu,
unburnt but sweetly singed.

Behind the lathe I found a 1946 *Sun-Telegraph*, one of Pittsburgh's
ten dailies, war over. Extended family moved West,
homes of lovely cream, they took shoes off
when entering, amassed tons of human capital

till 1969—were you among the millions who refused
grapes for three years? Do you
know what I'm talking about?
My chicory is stored in a can not

Maxwell House blue or Folgers red, but silver as the temples
of my teachers, who were self-taught, ivy-taught,
head-shot, lovelorn, lovesick; who were plagiarized, ripped
off walls by jealous students, jurors, colleagues, and *makhers.*

Who guided then buried me, deeper, in books.
We fucked our teachers, they fucked us over,
unable to leave.

II.

The memoir I won't be writing
attends lost writers, betrayals, inventions, and swerves
most no longer visit. My distinctions between autumn
and spring, metropolis and ex-urb, under nightfall's

blask/shine, mean to dim the paywalls. My time
in architecture stopped at land art, the Jetty
and the Orbital Reflector, the Fumarole, the binding of the Hague
(failed), hiker "cairns," "towers," "labyrinths," "petroglyphs,"

and "love notes." Once, on a mountain hike, I passed
Carve a tree/remember me/I was here/don't bury me.
Afterward, in a camp w/wireless, I let my pre-tween
great-nephews watch, then imitate, naked MOMA dancers,

slide like snakes across the cabin's porch flicking tongues at me,
swiveling then resting eyes on me. Instinct, art—both—
chasing me up and down the steps, unzipping my pack
and throwing cinnamon onto the fire pit? The flash burn was awesome!

III.

Beneath my quilt stains and re-knottings
I listen for you, into the night, dear Endymion—
"I speak in this tongue that will pass."
Baci's auburn knot revolves, Earth

rotates, calming, spinning me
inside flame-rings blue and pine-green.
All I know, having broken
my ankle and fainted, is hearing her

come running, tilting a pot of boiling water over the iced walk,
she makes waves of steam and I can stand a bit,
braced against her coffee-and-wool-coat smell.
"You have to know!" she shakes me from my thicket

between fields, I am swooning
under a caffeine lesson, flown to harvest
shades of tiny beans: citrine, peridot, on mats
the scarlet ripening,

nourishing her *kawa* soul.
Morning of August 24, 1954, before shooting himself
through the heart, last note of Getúlio Vargas
to the cartels: "I have given you my life.

I fear nothing. Serenely I take my first step
toward eternity and leave my life
to enter history. There is nothing
to give you except my blood."

Along the turnpike toward home, chicory, flowering.
Baci ground the roots to strengthen her supply.
Bitter and nut-buttery, digestive balm.
I never learned her thoughts of politics,

only wars. I say she sat in terror over TV news,
half-slept under the bloody hearts,
her son's portrait beneath the Christ's.
I read at her knee

while she combed my hair with her fingers.
Bookmarks she gave me: scrap of lace, scrap of eyelet,
once a tangerine peel, a shirt collar for the heavy dictionary.
Roots, threads, her every grammar, ornament.

DRYAD

—Diana Krall covering Joni Mitchell's "For the Roses," bootleg versions

Head-phoned, June dusk porch,
  I listen to the voice's magenta,

and voice behind it,
  twining vibrato of a woman's spine,

trembling rope of vertebrae,
  discs and fluid between them,

Krall locating then drawing sharp
  vespers down inside the lateral

canes of the floribunda,
  then outward, lifting shapes of trellises and walls

into night sky
  seething her cover
of Mitchell's uncanny fame dirge.

Her voice
  races and lashes distant California and far New York, sings:

Unfollow the creeds
to *circulate your soul around*
and be
Just you up there/getting them to feel.

Canopy feeds equally
on wood and water, honey, dirt,
and the roses' phosphorus burning green fire.

TERRARIUM

No sense
following light

or fuel, Father.
Both lead to new wars,

threads slip
narrowest places
running haywire.

Holding your arms out to me
six weeks after dying

holding the terrarium
you cut and fitted from old window glass
half a century earlier,

the sturdy box gleaming
in the dark beyond,

you'd mounded soil, measured
low hills and woods and fed them
lake water pumped through silver tubes,

a majestic
scaled display, making sure

I know.

FLORIBUNDA

Series of doors flipping, fanning
one into the next

sound of glass slides on a lab table,
smear of blood

then a corridor, stubby blue-lit
chute I slide through

to find my mother
eight days after

in a round
solarium, sunny on her walker

or will she tip over
into the white-hot alcove

her new form
touching the hand-grip

as one would lightly touch a sapling
in the woods.

I run my palm along
the scruffy rose-canes

edging the parking lot
where I wheeled her down

her last summer's narrow path
two blocks from the Atom Smasher,

Dad's *lararium*
for our household gods.

At the thruway's
waterfall, I hear her say

There's Lefty, and Stacey,
and our cousins under the Rzeszow

willow—Hold up—

I yell, lock the wheels,

face the eight-foot stalks'
green splays and thorns—

pink slashed cream-white
eyes darting, frantic, side to side

along the roses' stage.
I'm unaware I'm

starting to drift, crossing through
perfumes, watered silk, knives—

foundations of my denials.

WORDS TO A SPY

I didn't want you
looking at, let alone
writing about me. Hated

your brain shrine, male
gaze writing any woman
that clearly, smug,

seeing things
I couldn't, then.
Forget me—

your tone's off, your eye's
dull, but you nailed my teeth
and coffee stains.

My city gave you away.
You lost the details in plain sight:
her street angels and old-school
butchers. I know a woman tending

a bluejay cemetery
under a red spruce.
How would you write her,

bent over like that
entering shadows and temples?

QUANTUM BURN

If having achieved
your prognoses or purpose

you walk and vote correctly,
spend from the upper deck, not the belly

drink the six not six-plus ounces
of wine though yes wine is a biological

fluid and the infusions you will need
are biological and may interfere,

if you
upload and back-up

should the plan be rescinded in 20__
you will have been grandfathered in,

if you reach the correct
not the advanced directive Social

Security portal on or by 0X/0X/20__
if you've remembered to approach

enrollment of the first justice
since the abolitions.

But if
you were born with a womb
on the day of your younger brother's

younger sisters
it is for us

to bury you
and you to exhume.

REDWOOD

—for Anne Waldman

Now that the universes keep expanding
and can be viewed more psychedelically
through the Webb scope,
I return to
not a nothing from nothing
infinite birth, or big bang, but
a redwood

reclining, upended for a moment,
teaching me, common house-ant,
starting from its root ball,
broad as a few solar systems,
crawling the micro-hairs' winding path,
making assignments
up onto the main trunk

and in ten million or so years
I might reach a tablet
inscribed with the poems of Enheduana;
and in another stretch
a bark-cliff-edge leading inside the mind
of Dante, and so on. All while I watch
for companions, or wonder
what they're up to—

—that knot is my childhood village's
mysterious people, their talk and backstories;
—these cracks in the bark are channels
to the sky;
—the needles bring the dead through
electronics, this I know

and think of all the years I've been reading
you, dear Anne on your birthday,
reading you as I've always done, one book
at a time, keeping it in my bag for
weeks, often when traveling:

solitary transport
reading, re-reading, knowing
there's much more, of *Iovis*, or
Marriage, *Manatee*, *Bard*, or Insta's
Fast Speaking Music. Singing,
I court the ant:

This is your brain/
This is your brain on drugs/
and charting the age of a
universe is like
reading for pleasure
and wisdom, simultaneously.
Traveling the redwood

I recall an afternoon we took
a drive, I, mapless, looking

for a yarn shop specializing in worsted
sheep's wool fresh from the hands
of the Winooskie spinner. You were
excited with a new project, and somber
about the Archive, then we stopped
to look at a brook saturating
the road and stepped, happy, into our
splendid concentrations.

THE GRASSY KNOLL. THE BOX CUTTERS. READER NOTES.

Pavese's diary, 9th November, 1936:
He is excited by the workings of repetition in his new poems.

The present and past meet, he writes, by *mainspring*, which is image.

When I stayed in Santo Stefano di Belbo, I returned each morning to Nuto's doorway along the rail tracks; shop windows bearing Pavese's portrait; pharmacy; café; weekly to the bodego for another bottle of Barbera with the *La Luna e i Falò* lable I eventually steamed off as bookmarks; street installations bearing his poems, repeating to make sure I would forget nothing.

Repetition, *not for reasons of harmony but of construction*, he writes.

A first-year MFA student, I quickly dropped a seminar devoted to the work of James Wright, idiotically hating his voice that struck too close (I thought) to home. In time, the four poet Wrights (James, Charles, Jay, C.D.) by way of Pavese's *Hard Labor*, the Arrowsmith translation, revealed what I'd lost.

Notice those the key phrases [in the new poems] are always in the present, and the others converge towards it even when they are in the past, he writes.

If I type *grassy knoll*, past still informs the present. The single bullet theory, long dismissed, long upheld,
moves in time.

When I reach for a box cutter to open an Amazon sleeve, I carry fore-thought and reversal, renewed, Atta's men ripping the throats of flight attendants.

Pavese's wide-screen of shifting scenes, thoughts, and feelings, shine inside his poem "Displaced People"/*Gente spaesate* whose two weary workers far from home enter twinned yet delicately opposing reveries. The speaker adores his home created from rough earth; his friend thirsts for his home-dream, an erotic paradise.

Ear-witnesses on Dealey Plaza said they heard multiple shots ring out, perhaps coming from a "grassy knoll." Dallas pastorale seemed both respite and stopped-down time, a longer summer than one had imagined inside the Northeast on a mild November afternoon.

The knoll falls greenly through the constructions of assassination dirges, scoring acoustics of gunfire.

Pavese's early work is informed, in part, by his love for and translations of Melville and Whitman. I returned, by way of Whitman, to James Wright, the great poet of the Ohio Valley, and his Martins Ferry, 62 miles from my home.

Diary, 13th May, 1938:
Pavese calls his earliest poems "lax," and some of my Italian friends agree and regard them as "practice" for his novels. He returned often to, and was buried in, Santo Stefano, natal village now given over to the deconsecrated church-turned-institute; annual festa Pavese; and the noble street installations. Across decades of re-reading *Lavorare,* I feel the construction ringing through every sentence he later wrote.

In the novel *The House on the Hill*, city, village, cabin, casa, tent—every structure is a singing dwelling.

In the late poem "Earth and Death," Pavese addresses a "you," a one/thing/beloved/divinity in that same way that the untranslatable Quasimodo does.

Of which paradise, in truth, were Atta's men thinking when they pulled out box cutters? A displacement, in the wet web of memories, of their mothers' knives, eyes, arms, or the arms of imagined girls, virgins to whom they would forever be heroes?

Believing the ear-witnesses means that I hold my sense of public disbelief. That doesn't make me a conspiracy theorist.

Diary, 9th November, 1936:
The word of phrase that is repeated is nothing else but mainspring of [the] image, constructed from top to bottom like a scaffolding, the pivot enabling the imagination to revolve on itself and sustain itself like a gyroscope which exists only ***in the present*** [ital., Pavese's], *while it is in action, and then falls and becomes just a bit of iron.*

"Displaced People's" nighttime canvas is back-lit, stark, "at the rear of a tavern,/each of us alone in the smoky haze." The laborers long for the specificity of one image—hills. By day they are tired of "too much of the sea" and "colorless water [which] stretches fully away,/disappearing into air." The speaker's friend romanticizes hills of "wild fruit and flowers" and delights in "peeling/off that green skin and finding girls, more naked than fruit." The speaker constructs a plainer beauty: "vineyards men have sweated to build/on that scorched ground." Both men have embarked on erotic eye-screens, yet the poem ends on a single image: grapes. Fruit of labor, promise of wine. I fell hard, in Santo Stefano, in an electrifying dislocation and transmission. The street installations bear quotes from poems, and mark hills and roadsides where certain poems might have been first imagined.

Then came the four houses:

—the natal home on the main road:

—La Mora, where he did farm work; one of his first duties, told through a protagonist, was "to break branches for the fire and grind the coffee, (*The Moon and the Bonfires,* Flint translation, 68);

—Il Nido, the "palace" of a wealthy family, where art and music lived;

—La Casa di Nuto, house of *amicizia,* of Pavese's lifelong, profound friendship with Nuto, or Pino Scaglione, where the clock and the paper desk calendar remain stopped upon the time and date of Pavese's death in far Turin.

The four houses, I feel, seemed to lift and extend themselves from their three dimensions into me. Each amplifies the structure of my transatlantic reading, each steadies my thinking, gives me the feeling that "I seemed to have drunk wine and become someone else" (82)

It is never fully possible to be like or to know another writer. But re-reading, over five decades, might allow an immersion or an imagined transmission, a kinship.

Writing from exile under "house arrest," in Brancaleone for

"anti-fascist activity," Pavese fully understood that his protagonist in *The Political Prisoner/Prima che il gallo canti,* (W. J. Strachan, trans.) experienced relatively modest levels of freedom measured out in his weekly housekeeper's service, café visits, and letters to and from his sister, his only permitted correspondent. The real prisoner was the partisan in the hill above the village, a man who would be hunted down and killed.

My four houses transmute their shapes:

La Mora is the truck farm above the Allegheny River where my uncle bunked and worked, from the age of thirteen, where hogs were driven down Pig Alley to the slaughtering field on the river bank.

Il Nido, palace of art, lit by an alabaster lamp, evenings, behind lace curtains, is my piano teacher's house fitted for the children's recital in Spring. The party table is lit with a glass bowl of cherry punch.

The natal home, and the house of long friendships conflate and merge—indoors, before a small bookcase in winter, reading with my brothers. Outside, in all weathers, my eternal sublime.

Pavese called his portal to a sublime "La Gaminella," a "hill like a planet."

At the edge of our village is the stretched-out backbone whose spine is studded with a large green dome, a place, thus far protected, place of underground water, and weapons.

I.

II.

III.

THE GREEN RAY

—optical phenomenon sometimes observed at sea horizons

Have I done enough,
counting the blue steel thistle-flowers at my door,
and bowing to the Child Gertrude, 85, sightless,

bent, cooling her pies on the sill.
Have I visited Miro's Flemish imitations enough,
his tender creams and bronzes, bright-rubbed silk-grays and scarlet pipings,

loving him as much as/more than Rembrandt—hold that thought?
I thread the canal belts and rings, running low
on cash, soon returning across the North Sea to home,
but walk the shoreline one more time, ticking through the fields
of tulips, with their 400 years of slaughter
and indulgences, so I might see, finally,

the daystar's half-second
stuff of miracles.
Feeling younger, a needle punching, no longer sliding, through surfaces,

edge of the 90 islands, in mud and gravel,
I sit, wait.
Have I delayed my strangeness

or have I been, like Gertrude's dreambook,
an open secret splayed on my morning table,
spellbound by increments in the shapes of numbers or letters?

Holding my breath inside the sun's descent,
disc white-hot, sky-hovering.
See it descending, buttering,

watch it, close eyes a second, lids hot canopies,
helpless, shut to cool, open
and see—wait for it—

blue sea and lemon star
flare to vapor—

and there a heartless green   a bitter lime   a freezer-burnt

chartreuse tongue—swollen and seething
horizontally atop
the sea—
What is about to leave our lives
at brutal speed?
Easing my eyeballs, softer now,

see it once, you just about have it.
Or, think you see it and burnish to gold flames

later, in the telling. Telling of it your whole life, thrill undimmed.

NIGHTS OF THE 1209

—mid 1970s

Respect Shawn's Farrah Fawcett pic
taped to the strongbox,
respect all gay/bi/straight/queer/super-
straight out to take a look,
    us in our river dresses or freak flags,
    combs or chains, chiffons, leathers,
    depending on mood or Movement—

day-job cash-flush
I took my seat at the bar.
    Side glance, blade of sideburn,
    our eyebrows like fault-lines met, double-take,
I leaned fast and lit her blunt:

brushed the cut of her three-piece suit,
tight, lapels wide stage curtains
she stepped through—
Her name was JL and she encased me,
still high from the glorious Michigyn
mud ditches of wimmin's Woodstock.
I'd queued in the rain outside her tent
but never reached the portal—

she'd pierced anything, all,
on the canvas floor of *Tits&Clits.*
She archived the sweet secretions

and blood-dots, historic underpapers,
then folded it all up for good,
one more lost

commercial dream inside Lesbian Nation.
Now we sipped our whiskey, admiring
shot glasses in Shawn's bright mirror.
"May all imitators who'll come later
come," she laughed, we toasted
Shawn who protected us
with her bowie knife and Beretta

and the city cops she tithed to;
she who once vaulted bar
then pool table
separating a tender bulldyke
from a Maoist prig—

respect Tex's bodyguards'
3 a.m. sharp entrance,
splaying blackjacks. S/he raised a hand
to Shawn, cufflinks glinting business—
thus we were buzzed through
the double steel door, out.

I walk the cinder path of lovers,
couples, solos, ghastly exposed
cells of the bus stops wafting
steam onto the ruined goddess rivers.

AFTER AN ARGUMENT

Un-paired at dinner with friends,
later, at home, permitted:
ask three questions

or was it
tell three truths?
She said she'd
sing hers,
ease the blow, I hoped:

"There's a lake.
The water is moving.
We cannot stay still."

Her discontent,
was she bored,
leaving me? Left?

I would leave, re-
buy my parents' house
and someone (me)

would move there to
"hold down the fort."
But the house was dank,

rock garden a grave.
I tried to translate her riddle.

The lake must be Erie.
Moving water must be Niagara Falls—
we'd nearly gone over, once,
years ago, headed for disaster.

No answer.
A more planetary mind
was called for:

"Winter new moon your sharp tongue.
Butterscotch your favored sun."
She answered,
"Bones of arms, ropes of curls
thread the riptide and steady our craft."

THE BADGES

My father knew:

enter the garage,

peel off white booties,

drop jumpsuit outside the cellar door,

step inside then drop white undershirt

into the tub of bleach.

Drop the plastic 2x2-inch badge

bearing his face

and Westinghouse site name

into the bucket

of used up little dosimeter blister packs

we plucked back out

to play spies. A spy I played

strung white lights around the cellar door

while Father sat at his bench

drawing hydraulic tools

and safety hatches.

You remember Cannekin, 1971,

Father, the chimney's rock rubble

rocketed up, plummeted down?

Onto the Dnieper River and Khakovka Reservoir

a Russian missile hit Zaporizhzha reactor this morning,

two more strikes just now.

The collapse forms another rubble chimney

then firestorm,

rocks will burst and fly back up—

—poisoned flume—

Father

in your distant realm

come no closer

don't look down.

spinning back down into the pellet bin

also called Earth, called vapor.

LEVELS

Some save heirloom crosses
and rosaries

medals rubbed to blurred satin.

I possess five levels,
the largest a cool steel six feet

which can steady a bench
being fitted for new legs;

The smallest and my favorite,
the nine-inch Torpedo Aluminum 124.

Her tinted topaz bubbles
lit by fluorescein

monitor my vessels
and eyesight.

All five serve as my walking sticks
through the old reactors.

LITTLE FOX STOLE

How the brass clamp
fixed your mouth to tail,
eyes shining while she turned
and bent to hug me,
your red-brown fur
brushing her auburn hair.
All the night-club hours

you must have danced
and twirled, head spinning,
or the lights too hot
and she rested you on the back
of a banquette, all the dancers
admiring your lounging,
perfumed with bourbon and smoke.

My pathetic thought of a woodland
escape for you, blazing streams
rushing where I buried you. I've
thought of returning so many times,
unburying,

though I'd promised
the banks of Sulfur Creek, restored,
fresh with wild cherry and young willows
would feel familiar to you, even if

the sharp triangles of your perfect ears

or the thread-claws of your feet
or wet black eyes
are chewed to dust.
I should have carried you

to the cremation shrine
and brought your ashes home.
Instead of laying you down in the grass,
alone, snout facing East, tail unfurled
West to the brutal Ohio.

SUGAR TABLE (2)

Flies wiped their legs on silk French knots,
glided mocha-spill trails
and buried thoraxes into the cross-stitched

lattices hiding last candy shards.
Tiny Janus eyes
reflected kitchen and front doors,

neighbors still arriving with covered
dishes, days after repast,
all the clear and amber bottles rinsed.

Bleach has not revealed the ancient
white altar cloth I now rip into panels
for my cats' beds or my own shroud.

POLAROID RIFF

Slower than iPhone, faster than

waiting the developer's shop,

a child's toy—slide paper in, frame, shoot, the image

spits out. Having it processed elsewhere might

change everything. Once, retrieving

photos from the shop I saw a ghost

moving chairs from odd corners and once

a girl I didn't know holding something out to me.

I admire Esther Kinsky's work of walking across

and back London, foraging, ferrying out

of flea markets old Polaroid prints, loving

their pink and orange tints.

Fast, framing then quickly holding

willow trees in my palm, and wetlands

we once called swamps but they were shallower

than swamps, they were marshlands

and meadows with freshets and pools long

after Vernal Equinox.

spirit sheds

under the tree in the grove.

ABOARD THE EMPRESS

Now spring's first surges touch the trees,

birdcalls and new air rushing the rivers.

No sooner had you set one forepaw

onto the waffle-steel ramp of the clipper,

security footage began uploading onto screens

your sprint—startled by a truck's

backfire—to the highest deck, your failed attempt

to cross the water.

Screen grabs all over town posted

then shared you by hand

as if preening over first sonograms.

Mine   *mine*   I long for your kinship

Cold, after-rain smell running down the hills into the waters,
smell of wet wood, scent of the valleys.

You wedged all eighteen pounds of you
into a ten-inch narrows, crew caught you
with a long pole like a fishing rod, caged,
transported you to Game Land 187
in Luzerne's deep woods.

I love your stubby tail and un-regal name,
the dark gray bars on your legs
expand as you age and grow to 35 pounds.
Lip, chin, neck, and belly fur all white.

Stripes and spots on your ears' wild tufts

focus my eyes

and the thick ruff of a heaven

slashed with thunder—that sky, that sound

is yours, every hand, every face,

yours

beloved bobcat

who would tear my throat and rip my eye from its socket.

PLICA POLONICA

—matted braid, similar to dreadlocks, common in Poland since medieval times, either hairstyle or—frequently incorrectly diagnosed as—medical condition

If I braid them tightly, rub them with oil
and do not touch or wash them

until spring, coins will appear
beneath my seasoned pelt

and if a doctor comes to cut them off,
mimicking fear of vermin and disease,

I know he's jealous of my keratin
vault, thick as a beaver tail. I can't say

whether first hairs sprouting after chemo
bore curse or promise, but so far I've documented

seven colors, from elven white to cinder black,
and the night the city archers came to cull deer

from Frick Park, a doe sheltered under our apple tree,
munching calmly, shitting dozens of pellets onto

fruit I'd hoped to harvest.
Mooning and mouth-pulling, I scavenged

bits of her fur. Overnight, whether through rheumatic vision or craving wine, my braids grew eleven inches.

I.

II.

III.

CULT OF GRAPPA

I pour, then correct my coffee
with a rill of liquid light.

In this way I protect
                    my solitude,

mind,
one thing at a time.

Better, too, for gazing
into the hallway mirror's unrefracted welcome
for my dead who enter double, triple visions,

while I set a row of shot-glasses,
plus one for the lovely scholar I dined with, evenings, last summer,

whose silk hem I spilled
wine on. In her elegant Sienesian she spoke
of her fifteen-year project,

a new Bocaccio translation
abandoned now, but a hermitage, nonetheless, she said, a beloved

prison in which she'd learned strict
seclusion and reveled in a dozen heated love affairs

no one but her husband
understood, though she lamented
his going off, deep into the North, and joining

the cult of grappa. "Precisely the same
I'd done," she said, "a prison of moderation
and thirst. You perhaps understand this?"

I nod, tonight, solemn, feeling my own love's
long month away where she delights in her great-
niece's baby-babble while scratching

final edits on an acute Superior Court appeal.
Her return and our reunion will be tender
with re-immersion, and escape.

My dead barely recognize this street, all offices
and new construction. Daily the new dispensary
spews gummies and plumes, snaking the bus stop,

sliming the historic bronze manhole discs.
Unlikely the hemp President Lincoln enjoyed
smelled remotely like this modern skunk-pot,
    My dead want

one more sweet Thai stick. Hours distinguish dagger-
glints from their tiny glasses,

relaxing their way
back down inside the 600-acre park's
ample space for return—where

I have no idea, cradling
my thimble-full of bitter grape seed,
to release, open my soul.

TOMB OF UNKNOWNS

—Italicized phrases are drawn from The Geography of Strabo Book III, translated from Greek to English by H.L. Jones in 1924. Strabo (64 BCE-25CE) traveled through Italy and various Near Eastern regions, writing physical and political descriptions.

After wine strong enough for sword and blade
the tyrant Dionysius of Syracuse sneaked
into the bed-chamber and fouled the girls
that pre-nuptial night.

He *bid the girls waltz around unclad.*
He *let loose doves with cropped wings*
upon them in the midst of the banquets,
and then bid some of them,

shod with sandals that were not mates
(one high and the other low)
chase the doves around.
Underground fires smoldered

then birthed quakes,
underground flames braided versions
and codes, the floor of the girls'
room began to buckle,

The tyrant *paid the penalty after he*
went back and resumed his government.
How, Strabo, did he pay?
[His enemies] *poured out most of their wrath*

upon his daughters, for they first made them prostitutes,
and then strangled them, and then after burning their bodies,
ground up the bones and sank them in the sea.

Fires birthing quakes created obsidian,
fashioned for centuries into mirrors,
but the reflections have produced no witnesses.

Each mirror you pass, Strabo,
becomes part of your report,
accurate or not,
never avenged,

and reveals a girl, now *ash*
suited to the vine.

SLEEPWALKER

My brother locks himself
inside sleep so deep
he rises in the night

walks to the kitchen window
over the well, out to the porch
down barefoot onto the yard

past the two white pines
and quaking aspen, brittle
yet flourishing at the berm

two generations, tree that recalled
for our mother her romanticized
West; he approaches his horse

at the fringe of creek grasses
under moonlight. Crayfish
and mosquito nursery, do not

wake the sleepers.
Breath-sounds of the horse
untether and liquify boyhood's

morning work on his camp
surveying the length of Sulfur Creek,
secreting himself in the woods,

climbing to the bluet meadow
and his spot above the white-gold
eyes of the flowers. He bends

to a face, places one eye
then another onto that keyhole,
feels its periphery

stopping down on fibers, shadows, triple
fractures, slivers and figures of light—

first camera—

He has never feared or ignored
quicksand, windstorm, snakebite

or burning acid runoff
and like the child Ansel Adams,

who tumbled onto his back in an aftershock
a continent away in coastal California

he latches eyes with a star world
of explosions and departures.

THE STRIPED MAPLE

Unbraided,
parallel, your green-gray
stripes thick as elven pens

climb, writing on rain and wind.
Scored on wood-rope
your music calls

to all things change-ling,
sheltered in bark-
leather, thick,

the better to climb—
maybe
        reaching heavenward

is a furled curtain, threaded
and sturdy, but who know how to read
between the lines, into such heart?

GOOD AND BAD GOVERNMENT

Why, walking along the River Mon

do I mind-text mosaicist El Anatsui:

"Skip New York and Edinburgh,

come visit with your copper-wire circlets

and aluminum pull-tabs dripping their scarlet

paint onto our ghost-fires."

Come for art, also flick the switch

on our new lab's monster-eater

who will sift and eat all plastics in the sea,

re-purpose, spit back out bio-

pellets, tubes, lungs and eyes of

human, creature, plant.

Why do I write in the continuous present

disappearing like cursive, like slow-thought going, gone,

recall the booth-curtain's formal sliding sound

on metal sprockets, rows on rows

that pull down and click,

each vote a tongue.

Why confess I have ignorantly

mostly in the choice of magistrate

twice logged my votes based on

a neighbor's impressions of his son-in-law's

knee surgeon, yet missed

only one primary in my long life?

Good and bad, a young bear loose

from the Highland Park Zoo has saved a bird

drowning in the Allegheny. An hour east

the slobbering drills are slipping fingers

of uranium into Indiana Creek. Why

do I avoid completing my DNR

and drinking from the fountain in the chemo lab;

why ignore a civic call to kill

invasives in Frick Park

yet keep my ritual walks at dusk

not thinking of much but space litter

dropping under stars

and glinting onto Hood Canal's nuclear subs.

Our county clerk today

leaked files on behalf of antique Sunshine

Laws, good. Walking on roadsides, foot-grooves

in bridges, viaduct catwalks, river-rat narrows,

tree lawns dotted with fleabane,

crabgrass, shreds, bins; pausing

at the netted coral geranium under the streetlamp

to detonate the negative space

of my curse on the High Court's

blows cast down on us. In Sienna I stood struck

before Lorenzetti's Council of the Nine,

". . . cast time under an aesthetic spell,"

art historian Randolph Starn writes, relief

in secular ease within the chamber

off the severe piazza's grid. I ducked away

from the Nine to visit the mural's doctor

for tinctures; bought socks in the wool shop,

had my boots re-soled, kissed

the fingers of the languid muses

and flew home safe to pray

under a lamp's calm disinterest.

Across the Allegheny, Old Vanka's murals
guard the last century's contradictions
in cobalt, green, and red.
Blood swells the breasts of the Mothers:
the guns; the fire stacks
and judges, a worker cradling
a model of the church in his arms.
Angel Prudence whispers
be careful what you say
against the tyrants.

I call my civic presence
campanilismo, patriotism,
though lately I have visited my borough office
mostly to complain.

PEACH MELBA

That hoof kicking inside my flank
on waking, hungry, Monday, no bread
no butter even Minerva Bakery,
          closed—
and Pat, hurrying in, murmuring,
laughing at the weather, 11 a.m. and it's already 88
degrees, no one knows she's dying, she's dancing
the room, waving a new poem in that way she has
and "Let's make Peach Melba!"
Drive to the co-op, windows down, her pink
Chevy's wings cranked. For her genius
idea I'm gifting her a doll head and skirt
I fashioned from my backyard hollyhock
and hoping the Chambersburg peaches
aren't sold out. Bins bursting, bag gently,
fly to freezers for French vanilla,
frozen raspberries will do, risk

ruining the Original and run

for heavy whipping cream, the door

opens, hushes closed,

misted then clear—

*

White night, white night

she'll climb three flights to her desk

bearing July's silver bowl of clouds and ice.

AUGUST NOISE

I'm thinning aisles of lemon balm
when Steve returns from the alley,
quiet, "I heard this is kind of
a witchy thing, I mean so much of it
in such a small yard, middle of the city,"
balm fronds brushing his knees.
He's refilled our rat bait boxes,
shakes spruce needles and a bee
from his burnt-red beard. "Witchy."

He means a compliment, glances
at my porch and screen door. What are
you looking for, I think of asking: crystals,
yowling fur-storms, more women—did you
know it's a calmative, also a pussy-sweeting
douche, tell your girl? But minding the gap, I point,

"What do you see?"
The *chelone obliqua/*turtle flowers' dark pink
heads fête the last days of summer.
"Pink flowers?" he says, finishing his paperwork.
The tortoises stand up in the heat,
guard my old excavation site of Zemmer
medicine bottles and a Seneca adze
I found then re-buried.

Steve gives me a thumbs-up, heads to his truck.
I tell him I eat onions like candy and screek at
bluejays consulting the daymoon. Pray we
protect the oikos without a gun.
I drop my baggie of dead lantern flies into the trash.

TO THE RAIN

Open my veins and arteries,
I don't know the difference.

Under the plane trees,
glaze me as I cross the river

wetted by good sky smell
before I enter

the nave to see Ludovica again.
I'm paying closer attention

this time, angle of her head thrown back
directly beneath the attic room

where Francis laid his head on his stone pillow.
Her marble-spun levitation

caresses her embroidered mattress, surely
damp, salted,

the bronze merely an assurance against
the long damp of the ageing church,

her mouth, dress, breath, thighs
contract so her orgasm is extending

and speeding the centuries
to and beyond

this moment, rain,
naked voice I'm listening to

drumming the roof
rivening the Tiber's surge.

Adolescent again,
I'm surprised by my body's

near-misses, luck,
and the new passageway

your voice allows.
Your celestial

time and ecstasy
surely surpass hers

and make death easier?
Merely a woman

who gave most of her wealth
to the poor, she is beatified,

but not
canonized (a wife, so clearly

not a virgin?), feast day January 31,
icy season

when your veins
are mighty enough to crack

rock and run
under Earth.

THE PAVESE STONE

—at Cortemilia

May we walk back to the bus,
ride back to the edge of Cava Alice's shelf

and grasses where the ancient African plate
slid north into the Piedmont?

So many grooves, barely wide enough
for a finger trailing the crevasses,

and the mud, the under-sea's
belly busy with solitary corals

digging tunnels up and into sandstone
pools. Dear spirit,

here is a ring I would slide onto your finger,
a plain thread.

Say two brief lines from *Leuco*
or *The Moon and the Bonfires;*

I've prayed to the sun-blazed hole
in the front barn wall at La Mora,

may I slip a letter or poem through
and no longer treat it

as the eye of a strange god?
Don't rush, please, I would have whispered

to the quarry men, don't cut
so fast, but they split clay,

hoisted, settled the slab
onto the flatbed for you

who would not settle—only arrive.
I took the north bus, stepped off and walked

as if bearing a stranger
into Cimitero S. Stefano Belbo,
stopped while the men smoked,
lifted, breathing, lowering

the slab onto your massive
fresh rectangle. I left my loves

though their neurons might
drift onto the damp earth.

I breathed the Alta Langhe
hazelnut dust, at home

with your sentient stone, most
beautiful. Its colors

are perfection, no powdered
ground or burnished ochre carries more

raw gold. No rust as rich a blood
no finer charcoal-stroke.

Your somber face,
eyeglasses, suspended pen

mapping waterways and trains.
Looking into your face I keep

blending our two cities, two wars, a third,
two voices I can't stop repeating.

I re-read you, walking into town
as if I'd been dropped or slid into it

whole, from girlhood when I first
tried writing, taking photos

with an empty camera.
When Natalia Ginzburg wrote

you were a difficult friend
I raised my hand immediately:

That's me, too! When I read
you I wait for you at the bar

in case you might show,
disappearing all the myths

though you usually drink your cup
with first sun, and I tend to sleep late.

NOTES

"The Owls of Piazza della Rotonda"—italicized excerpts are from Percy Bysshe Shelley's poem "The Aziola."

"Sugar Table" — "Stoney" refers to Stoney's beer, first brewed in Smithton, Pennsylvania in 1907.

"The Grassy Knoll. The Box Cutters. Reader's Notes"—italicized excerpts are from Cesare Pavese's *The Burning Brand, Diaries* 1935-1950, translated by A.E. Murch. Walker and Company, 1961.

"Good and Bad Government"—El Anatsui's internationally admired work makes use of recycled bottle-and-can-top assemblages, forming cloth-like wall sculptures.

In the poems "Words to a Spy," "Aboard the Empress," and "To the Rain," I have imitated, and offered variations on, a few phrases from poems by Salvatore Quasimodo.

ACKNOWLEDGMENTS

I am grateful to the editors of the following journals, in which some of the poems appeared or are about to appear, some in different versions or under different titles:

Italian Americana, John D. Calandra Italian American Institute—"Words to a Spy," Maria Terrone, poetry editor.

On the Seawall—"Redwood," Ron Slate, editor.

A Literary Field Guide to Northern Appalachia—"Striped Maple," Todd Davis and Noah Davis, editors.

Prairie Schooner—"The Owls of Piazza della Rotonda," "The Tube," "Along the Juniata," and "The Sugar Table," Timothy Schaffert, editor.

*

My gratitude to Marisa Frasca, Alessio Rotundo, Michael Simon, Marie Sauret, Anne Marie Macari, Mary Taylor Simeti, Rosanne Bérubé, Frances Baker, Stephani Flom, Robin Becker, Erjola Tafaj, Janice Anderson, the Real Wildsisters, Shannon Sankey, Sean Nevin, Lisa Alexander, Katherine Steinmetz, Kristin Mellon, Katherine Homrok, Saad Sheikh, Alexander Olawaiye, and Pascal Zinn.

And heartfelt thanks to Jan Beatty, Toi Derricotte, Lawrence Joseph, Geeta Kothari, Ron Wallace, Mihaela Moscaliuc, and Michael Waters.

Travels to remote places in western Pennsylvania, the Adirondacks, eastern Poland, and northern Italy contributed to my understanding of connections between them all.

Finally, thank you to my editor Carey Salerno for her intense eyes and hearing inside this work, and to everyone at Alice James Books for their patience and hard work.

RECENT TITLES FROM ALICE JAMES BOOKS

A Holy Dread, R. A. Villanueva
The Palace, Andrés Cerpa
Let the Moon Wobble, Ally Ang
The Seeds, Cecily Parks
All the Possible Bodies, Iain Haley Pollock
Saint Consequence, Michael M. Weinstein
Freeland, Leigh Sugar
Mothersalt, Mia Ayumi Malhotra
When the Horses, Mary Helen Callier
Cold Thief Place, Esther Lin
If Nothing, Matthew Nienow
Zombie Vomit Mad Libs, Duy Đoàn
The Holy & Broken Bliss, Alicia Ostriker
Wish Ave, Alessandra Lynch
Autobiomythography of, Ayokunle Falomo
Old Stranger: Poems, Joan Larkin
I Don't Want To Be Understood, Joshua Jennifer Espinoza
Canandaigua, Donald Revell
In the Days That Followed, Kevin Goodan
Light Me Down: The New & Collected Poems of Jean Valentine, Jean Valentine
Song of My Softening, Omotara James
Theophanies, Sarah Ghazal Ali
Orders of Service, Willie Lee Kinard III
The Dead Peasant's Handbook, Brian Turner
The Goodbye World Poem, Brian Turner
The Wild Delight of Wild Things, Brian Turner
I Am the Most Dangerous Thing, Candace Williams
Burning Like Her Own Planet, Vandana Khanna

Alice James Books is committed to publishing books that matter. The press was founded in 1973 in Boston, Massachusetts to give women access to publishing. As a cooperative, authors performed the day-to-day undertakings of the press. The press continues to expand and grow from its formative roots, guided by its founding values of access, excellence, inclusivity, and collaboration in publishing. Its mission is to publish books that matter and preserve a place of belonging for poets who inspire us. AJB seeks to broaden our collective interpretation of what constitutes the American poetic voice and is dedicated to helping its artists achieve purposeful engagement with broad audiences and communities nationwide. The press was named for Alice James, sister to William and Henry, whose extraordinary gift for writing went unrecognized during her lifetime.

Designed by Zoe Norvell

Printed by Versa Press